Table of Contents:

Introduction

Dear Reader,

In the night, already in bed, with external distractions largely eliminated, the beginning of this introduction flows through my mind. The following morning, if not written down, it may be a wasteland, all being forgotten, with no fragment remaining.

So it is often with the surfacing of poems. If this happens at night, I usually get up to write the lines down, for if I wait until morning, they are usually gone and cannot be retrieved. If, during the daytime, a poem's subject introduces itself, I usually go to the computer immediately and begin writing.

There are long periods, days, even weeks, when not a single new poem comes to life. Then there are other times when I have, what I call, poetic diarrhea. One poem after another pops into my mind asking to be completed. There's no stopping. And the subjects range from simple recounting of past memorable events to the pondering of what has been, what is, and what is yet to be.

By now I have written more than four hundred poems, and with this issue self-published four hundred in two volumes. I must also have translated from German to English about six hundred poems of three authors. Added to this are the translations and publication of novels, novellas, and short stories by the popular German writer, Karl May, in a total of seventeen volumes, plus the biography of Isabell Steiner.

Also, there's my autobiography written in 2004, and the biography of my wife's grandparents and parents who were Lutheran missionaries in Sumatra. Once completed in 2001, I translated this biography from English – my preferred language, spoken for two thirds of my life – to German, and my sister-in-law with her husband in Berlin are completing it with additional material, transforming it into good German which, through the years, has somewhat escaped me.

Lastly, there are the numerous travelogues and science articles I have written and published.

But back to *Pondering What Is*. More so than the poems in *Observations And Reflections*, the following collection is more personal, often dealing with the trials and tribulations that have arisen in my later years. However, as in my first publication, I could not omit including my two favorite poems at the end of this issue, Karl May's *Spirit* and Rudyard Kipling's *If*.

May you appreciate them as I still do.

Herbert Windolf   Prescott, Arizona

Sublime

Geology, most rough and tumble,
built and eroded manifold,
formations great and ever changing,
through eons, unimaginably long,
which, for us humans, ephemeral,
are most stunning to behold.
In Arizona's north, near Utah's border,
a meandering sandstone tops it all.
It's called the Wave,
its layers curving, bending, rising,
sublime they are,
a wave of stone.

The greatest shortcoming of the human race
is our inability to understand the exponential function.
Albert A. Bartlett

Passages,

of which there are many,
through time and also space.
From childhood to the teens,
to adulthood and old age.
From youth's drive and confusion
to maturity,
and with luck,
to grace.
In the course of these years
we may travel afar
to at last arrive at this distant place,
from where we no longer depart,
through time and space.

No race can prosper till it learns that there is as much dignity in
tilling a field
as in writing a poem.
Booker T. Washington

Asteroids

Aplenty there are,
in the tens of thousands,
small and huge.
Most orbit far out
between Jupiter and Mars.
But some are erratic,
they cross the Earth's path,
and in time's course
will impact to leave their mark.
Worse are the comets,
from the Oort Cloud ejected,
which come out of nowhere,
and can't be expected.
In the past it rarely mattered,
too few of us were around.
But today's civilization
is fragile at best,
and a larger collision may come at great cost.
We must get together
and plan for what's coming,
if not soon, then in future,
to overcome this force of Nature.

The optimist proclaims we live in the best of worlds;
and the pessimist fears it is true.
James B. Cabell

Coherence

is what makes a good mind,
the ability to assemble
what is of a kind.
To disregard extraneous matter
and focus on that which counts,
not the scatter.
Alas, how many practice this art,
how many a mind is trained
and that smart?
Most of us
just muddle along,
only a few realizing
where they failed or went wrong.

Two things are infinite:
The universe and human stupidity;
and I'm not sure about the universe.
Albert Einstein

Incoherence

the lack of clarity
in thought and speech,
so often amiss in communication.
Then, when it's received,
twisted and filtered by anticipation,
and not perused with proper attention,
one marvels how we ever succeed,
and that we manage to agree.
And it is not too rare
that one or the other
of the talkers in case,
is of his misinterpretations
not even aware.

When people talk, listen completely.
Most people never listen.
Ernest Hemingway

5

Friendship,

cultivated, is precious and true,
and second to good marriage,
rightfully due.
It calls on our friends
to accept who we are
and to cherish the things
on which we agree.
Then, where we differ,
respect our friends
and, at times, disagree
to question our partners different stand.
But, last not least,
when need calls for,
to stand by our friends
for support and succor.

One friend in a lifetime is much, two are many,
three are hardly possible
Friendship needs a certain parallelism of life,
a community of thought,
a rivalry of aim.
Henry Brooks Adams

Law of Unintended Consequences

We strive and we venture
with the best plans in mind,
yet Nature is complex
as we often find.
We aim for a goal
seemingly simple and straight,
only to realize
that the outcome achieved
is quite different
from the goal we had in mind.

That's what all we are. Amateurs. We don't live long enough
to be anything else.
Charles Spencer Chaplin

Culture

What does it take to create a culture,
then what is required to make it last?
It requires a set of customs shared,
and what's more important,
a strong belief
about life and death,
a deity who created it all,
and, last not least,
a story how the world was made.
This lies at the root
of all human cultures.
It binds them together,
makes them one and strong.
But once this belief
does fizzle and fade
the culture, too,
most likely has seen
its better days.

Imagination is more important than knowledge.
Knowledge is limited.
Imagination encircles the world.
Albert Einstein

Friendship 2

How peculiar is American culture
to call everyone a "friend"
one has seen a few times,
but that's where it ends.
If it goes any further,
he becomes a "good friend,"
but for the former
the term of "acquaintance"
is rarely meant.
There is some appeal
in that quick acceptance,
but the question arises:
does it bridge any distance?

It takes only a minute to get a crush on someone,
an hour to like someone,
and a day to love someone –
but it takes a lifetime to forget someone.
Unknown

Terminal Friend

Granite Brown,
you dear old friend,
you made it to ninety,
but as you know very well
even granite turns into sand.
Congratulations, good man!
What enjoyment we had,
on our walks in Provence,
in Arizona, Lake Tahoe and in the Harz.
We skippered the Rhine,
had a glass of wine.
In Munich you loved the knuckles and salad,
you always remembered as being so fine.
In Goslar you checked for a train to get home,
just in case, by chance, I wouldn't return.
All that we'll remember
in the years yet to come,
until we follow you
into the setting sun.

When life gives you a hundred reasons to cry,
show life that you have a thousand reasons
to smile.
Unknown

Globalization 1

We will come together
in a global civilization,
kicking and screaming,
whether we want it or not.
For if we don't
we will fail as a species
and will never be able
to fulfill our wants.

The trouble about man is twofold. He cannot learn truths which
are too complicated;
he forgets truths which are too simple.
Rebecca West

Murmurations

There's the eloquent movement
of swarms of sardines,
attempting to escape their pursuers.
There are the hundreds of thousands
of African Quelea
which, on their migration, darken the sky.
But most beautiful is
the exquisite dance of as many starlings,
their clouds of bodies,
which, in unison, paint the dusky heavens
before they settle in for the night.
Their beating of wings,
their rush through the sky,
makes a murmuring sound,
back and forth, as they fly.

That which yields is not always weak.
Jacqueline Carey

Blaming

It is oh so easy
to blame someone else,
for a trouble one is feeling.
Victim,
it spells!
Responsibility
for one's actions
shunted to the back of the mind
will forever hold it back,
keep it shackled,
in bind.

If you don't control your mind,
someone else will.
John Allston

Fred

There once was this friend,
a baker by trade.
We did a few things together.
Older than I,
his heart gave out,
and off he went
to meet his maker.
The years have gone by,
I remember him still,
by something we had in common.
It was apple fritters we loved.
At times, when I got one for myself,
a second one was for him from the shelf,
we then devoured together.
So, these days,
when I pick up one,
then eat it in my car,
I do remember my friend.

Happiness is not something you experience,
it is something you remember.
Oscar Levant

Projecting,

a "game" played by many folks
who do not listen well.
Anticipating a speaker's words,
before he is done,
they have read his mind,
no matter whether they are wrong or right.
An irritant in conversation,
they are the scourge of understanding.

In a mad world,
only the mad are sane.
Akiro Kurosawa

Soul

No, not the religious kind,
the one's supposed to live forever.
It is an immaterial force,
ethereal, yet powerful
in animating personal fervor.
Intense and sensitive, emotional,
it dwells deep inside everyone,
it powers our very being,
sometimes it slumbers,
sometimes, emotionally, comes to the fore.
It's not accessible to reason,
its roots do dwell in childhood, deep.
Both, good and bad,
it is the personification,
the very making of our soul.

Each of us bears his own Hell.
Virgil

Forgiveness,

oft so difficult to grant
for injury and wrong that's done.
It's usually of a personal nature,
but can be on a social scale,
as done to Jews by Germans,
and Africans by Westerners.
The victims, individuals and groups,
may suffer in the years to come,
some never try, some overcome.
If not addressed, it festers on,
and not all wounds are healed by time.
But once resentment ceases towards the offender,
or when the perpetrator realizes what he's done,
then comes the chance for its atonement,
and for forgiveness for a future time.

Not everything that is faced can be changed,
but nothing can be changed until it is faced.
James Baldwin

Canoeing

Often I paddled the lakes up north,
the Boundary Waters and Quetico.
The lakes so peaceful,
the forests vast,
the bears and fishes I barely saw.
Blueberries, tasty and plentiful,
cooking fires I always kept small.
Portages were sometimes long,
with mosquitoes waiting for me to come.
But fondly I remember
the closeness to and immersion in nature.

In the end, it's not going to matter
how many breaths you took, but how
many moments took your breath away.
Shing Xiong

Vignettes

are what I call my poems,
brief, to the point reports.
Together with the many subjects
and their supplementing mottos
invite the reader's further thought.
It's not my style
to dawdle and diddle.
I'd rather play my middlin' fiddle.

Never mistake knowledge for wisdom.
One helps you make a living;
the other helps you make a life.
Sandra Carey

Limerick

There once was this kid from a little town
who ventured into the world.
He tried and strove and in the end,
he thought he had it made.
But lo and behold,
when all was done,
he found he had after all failed.

Time is a great teacher,
but unfortunately it kills all its pupils.
Hector Berlioz

Glorious

We rafted twice the Colorado,
the canyon walls to left and right.
Grand were these towers and their colors,
the waters tinted reddish bright.
The rafts were powered just by oars,
eleven days we went,
the rapids' rush, Lava Falls' roar,
excited us like naught before.
The nights benign in early fall,
star-speckled was the sky,
though narrowed by the canyon's walls,
the constellations shone so bright.
We hiked the canyons to the side,
saw water tumbling from up high,
swam in the waters clear and cold.
It was adventure great and bold.

What would life be like if we had no courage to attempt
anything?
Vincent van Gogh

Testosterone

the drive of Life
is found across all species.
Without, no striving and no competition
would have all creatures driven on
to better their genetic tone.
But double-edged a sword it is,
producing violence,
death in extremis.
It carries,
like so much in life,
two sides
we humans have to weigh,
and for a balance need to strive.

Whoever fights monsters should see that in the process
he doesn't become a monster.
Friedrich Wilhelm Nietzsche

Missionary

There was this Lutheran missionary
who ventured into the Wilds.
When once traveling his outlying territory,
he came upon a heathen tribe.
The village was in deep distress,
a little boy had died.
The women wailed and tore their hair,
the men beat drums and cried.
He had an elder still the noise,
then told the listening crowd:
If you were Christians
you'd have no need
to despair about your loss,
for you would find your boy in Heaven again
and once more be together, thus.
Much later, I couldn't hold back my surmise:
When he gets there, will he be surprised!

He who knows does not speak;
he who speaks does not know.
Tao The Ching

Aphorisms

I love these statements,
concise as they are.
A thought oft condensed in one sentence.
This is why I cite them
after each of my poems,
to supplement, amplify, or counterpoint
as enhancement.

An aphorism ought to be entirely isolated from the surrounding
world
like a little work of art
and complete in itself like a hedgehog.
Friedrich von Schlegel

Dope

Why do some people want to get high,
or dopey, as is the matter?
Is their inner life so impoverished, poor,
that they need to enhance
or to dull it?
There is plenty in real life
to explore and to venture
that escape is useless,
an existential failure.

Everybody wants happiness,
nobody wants pain.
But you can't have a rainbow
without a little rain.
Unknown

Quiet,

so very welcome,
with noise everywhere
that is dulling the senses
in our modern world.
I would love just to hear
the wind in the trees,
the croak of a raven,
the song of a bird,
against the chatter of TV,
so terrible in airport lounges heard.
The blaring of radios,
the ring of phones,
the roar of a jet,
the noise of machines.
If only one could
turn these darn things off,
and for better or worse,
regain precious peace.

Many people say it is insane to resist the system,
but it is actually insane not to.
Mumia Abu Jamal

Illumination

At night, in bed,
when darkness calms the senses,
the mind is enlightened,
the spirit soars,
thoughts do flourish,
ideas are tossed about,
and lines of poems rise and tumble.
These are the times when lyrics call,
demanding that one write them down,
for if one fails to heed them then,
they fade, are gone,
by morning's dawn.

There is no reality except the one contained within us.
That is why so many people live such an unreal life.
They take the images outside of them for reality
and never allow the world within to assert itself.
Hermann Hesse

Themes

There is a friend,
a poet, too,
who's run out of subjects to address.
But life's so full of themes and problems
there is no shortage of new topics.
From deep inside they often rise,
best when emotion is their drive.
The intellect does have its role,
the best of poems, though,
are powered by the soul.

It's only words . . .
unless they're true.
David Mamet

Life

We probe the universe for life,
here, "other" being of importance.
The life on Earth is of one kind,
we are related,
siblings of each other,
but all too often do forget,
and not respect or just don't bother.
Despite this plenitude of our kind of life,
we want to learn:
Are we alone?
Did "other" life arise somewhere?
Are we just one of many forms?
Whatever we eventually find,
it will be staggering to our mind.
But should we learn
we are alone,
by God
would this not tell us some?

Its not what I had feared,
but what I had not thought to fear.
Edgar Allan Poe

Sequoia sempervirens

Always green,
they rise to the heavens,
the tallest trees on Earth.
Whoever has walked these sequoia groves,
those that escaped the lumberman's saw,
remembers them forever.
Oh, the stillness, the peace,
rarely broken by the chirp of bird or squirrel,
or the gurgling of a brook.
Some live two thousand years or more,
imagine what all they could tell.
Compared to them
we are but a blink in time,
beings, utterly ephemeral.

Millions long for immortality
but do not know what to do with themselves
on a rainy afternoon.
Susan Ertz

earth

colloquially known as dirt,
demeaned by this word,
but only because,
when handling it,
it leaves hands dirty.
Yet a thimble full
is so rich in life.
That's why we should cherish
the earth of our Earth,
for without it,
we would not be alive.

In the end, it's not going to matter
how many breaths you took,
but how many moments took your breath away.
shing xiong

Bach

Johann Sebastian,
as he is known,
wrote music sublime and profound.
It is told that he once said
that the music he wrote
was for the enjoyment of man
and the glory of God.
Yet, in his Orchestral Suites,
Suite 2, number 6,
the very last set,
he composed a piece
in which he playfully met
a brook's gurgling,
a most happy sound,
in which piccolo flutes
most joyfully abound.

The ultimate measure of man is not where he stands in
moments of comfort
but where he stands at times of challenge and controversy.
Martin Luther King, Jr.

Exit

There once was a friend,
eighty-six years of age,
diagnosed with terminal esophageal cancer.
He opted against
radiation and chemo,
and rather faced his end.
He no longer ate,
drank only water,
called in his friends,
a pair at a time.
And for awhile,
at their minimal lunch,
he joined them and said his good-byes.
Within a few weeks
his goal was met,
a kind and dignified exit.

When one door closes another door opens;
but we often look so long and so regretfully
upon the closed door
that we do not see the ones which open for us.
Alexander Graham Bell

Sandstone

laid down through eons
by deserts in millions of years.
Windblown their layers,
eroded, compounded,
cross-bedded, time compacted them.
Arizona's north and Utah's south
hold the most gorgeous formations.
Go see them before your time runs out,
their beauty, made for the ages.

If we could read the secret history of our enemies
we should find in each man's life
sorrow and suffering enough
to disarm all hostility.
Henry Wadsworth Longfellow

Deliberateness

Dogs, so loyal,
are full of emotion.
Cats are deliberate,
they parse their devotion.

Great minds think alike . . .
fools never differ.
Unknown

Vitality

Some people have it,
many don't.
Some go from task to task
creating,
while others, consuming,
never won't.
Where do the few gain the energy from,
to engage and produce,
to go on and on?
Are they differently wired,
were they differently raised?
Is their physique simply stronger,
or were they by Nature
simply better apprised?

Genius is the ability to reduce the complicated to the simple.
Chinese proverb

Memorial

When rememb'ring a person
we tend to be kind,
and laud the departed
for what all he did
and left behind.
We extol his virtues,
or hers, for that matter,
and lavish on praise,
leave nothing in tatters.
But no one is perfect,
there sure was some failing,
should there not be truth, too,
in our lauding and praising?

If you must chose between two evils,
pick the one you've never tried before.
Unknown

Narrative Poetry

It's accepted, it's modern, it's everywhere,
but to tell you the truth:
I don't really care.
I can't process the stories,
the verbal onslaught,
I lose track of what's said,
fall asleep over it.
I'm not demented,
but very much do I like
that info presented
is cogent and tight,
which is why my poems
must be seen in this light.

Being sad with the right people is better
than being happy with the wrong ones.
Philippos

Gold

A few years ago
when the world seemed to end,
with the economy crashed,
people buying silver and gold,
I went au contraire
and sold all my gold.
I made some good profit,
why would I hold on,
let optimists rule,
when pessimists run.

Laughter is the antidote to existential pain.

S. Spencer Baker

Technology

There are many who believe
that technology
will cure our ills,
but they should take into account
that technology
all too often also kills.
If we keep on going
as we presently are,
with computers and robots
becoming ever smarter,
then, in the decades to come,
to find good jobs will become
ever harder and harder.
More people will get on the government's dole,
few being happy with this leisurely role.
For they won't know what to do
with all that time on hand,
few having the education
for a life well spent.

If you don't stand for something,
you'll fall for anything.
Unknown

Garbage

In the early eighties we stayed on Tobago,
one day found remote Bloody Bay,
its name derived from a naval fray,
whose casualties had tinted this beautiful bay.
We walked the beach,
which was littered with garbage,
most likely tossed overboard from ships.
And in 2014 when satellites scoured the Indian Ocean,
in the hope of finding MH370 remains,
they spotted uncounted pieces of trash,
this, not a single reporter to bemoan.
Then there's the Pacific Gyre,
where plastic galore does float forever.
And space, too, is littered with plenty of garbage,
dangerous to pass through or there to be.
If we do go on producing this litter,
we'll be drowning in garbage
we so shamefully produce,
and even worse to behold, to see.

It is not what you look at,
but what you see.
Thoreau

Strutting

Strutting, we walk the stage of life
ignorant of much there is.
We try and try to understand,
yet fail in our enterprise.
We catch a glimpse
of what it's all about,
only to miss the larger context
and remain, as it is,
in a fog or a cloud.
But that's all we can do.
Only a few of us will
accomplish the impossible
to find insight and peace
before we are called
from this endless mill.

Liberty means responsibility.
That is why most men dread it.
George Bernard Shaw

Samuel Gompers

Who still knows this man?
The founder of the A.F.L.,
the American Federation of Labor.
Years ago, he is said to have written:
What is it that Labor wants?
More schools, fewer jails,
more books and less guns,
more learning, less vice,
more leisure, less greed,
more justice, less revenge.
His request is forgotten.
by a doctrinaire free-market capitalism,
when, what is called for
is American pragmatism.

In a society without social justice and with a free-market
ideology,
guns, greed, and jails are bound to win.
Freeman Dyson / 1997

43

Sensing

How come
we sometimes sense
what is going to happen?
While I don't hold much coin in ESP,
I keep wondering what enables us?
Is it simply empathy?

Minds are like parachutes,
they only function when open.
Thomas Dewar

Germany

I come from the land
of the Denker and Dichter,
the thinkers and poets,
it once was called.
Then, something happened,
most terrible, ghastly,
it's almost impossible to behold.
Millions of people were killed in ovens.
Where then were the thinkers and poets
to shout and to act
and put this crime
against themselves and humanity
to an immediate stop?
I cannot make up for
what was done by my people,
but remain loyal for better or worse.
And what other peoples have done
is theirs to deal with.
It's not for me to judge and condemn,
yet also not to condone.

The books that the world calls immoral
are the books that show the world
it's own shame.
Oscar Wilde

Self

I keep wondering how we perceive our self?
Is it only confined to us humans
or who else?
There are some creatures
who recognize themselves,
in a mirror upheld,
and they know it is they,
and not someone else.
Most others, like cats,
don't give a hoot,
their recognition is nil,
their reaction mute.
But when we touch
or when we pet,
are we not addressing the self instead?
Are we then not reinforcing a sense of self,
the being's recognition
of its very own self?

The greatest good you can do for another
is not just share your riches,
but reveal to them their own.
Benjamin Disraeli

Taking Care

It's what most of them do –
mothers and wives –
taking care
of the essentials of life.
I'm not able to list
what all they do,
what all they accomplish
without much ado.
Men are no match for them by far,
mothers and wives,
caretakers they are.

The world is full of willing people;
some willing to work,
the rest willing to let them.
Robert Frost

Red Man's Revenge

The American Indian
was mistreated and hunted,
killed by diseases and the gun.
Treaties were broken,
his lands occupied,
his children were taken,
and he was kept on the run.
Reservations he was eventually given
were usually on marginal land
where he eked out a miserable life,
with alcohol always on hand.
Some of the tribes did better than others,
especially those living closer to towns.
They've now built casinos
for the Whites to gamble,
to take their money
for a better life.

Who controls the past controls the future;
who controls the present
controls the past.
George Orwell

Ravens

do waddle on the ground,
are almost funny earthbound.
But, lo, once they soar up into the sky,
use updrafts to cavort and play,
they are a joy to watch, to behold,
to envy their freedom,
and their dives, so bold.
Smart, they are, too.
Oh, to be such a bird,
not being earthbound,
not tied to the land.

Dream as if you'll live forever.
Live as if you'll die tomorrow.
James Dean

Defensive-Aggressive 1

some people are.
Much that they hear
draws their ire for sure,
which calls to defend
their persona, so poor.
And since they so easily feel put upon,
they respond with aggression,
their only tune.
They are hard to deal with,
if they could only be told:
It's alright, it's alright,
you are fine as you are.

How much more grievous are the consequences of anger
than the causes of it.
Marcus Aurelius

Hype

Most media love to dwell on it,
rich fodder for the masses.
And video games delight in killing,
and if not that then utter mayhem.
Why do the lowest human actions
find this intense appeal?
Why are suppliers of these features
catering to these actions, so unreal?
They feed the lowest common denominator,
and it's the money they are after.
The "good" works usually in silence
and must be boring to the mindless.

Maybe this world
is another planet's Hell.
Aldous Huxley

Rice

the food of millions,
much more so than maize and wheat.
What would the world be without it?
What other staple would there be to eat?
We are on these three grains reliant,
without them billions would be in great need,
for amaranth, buckwheat, barley, millet and oats,
quinoa and wild rice,
among several others,
are much too few
for those billions to feed.

The test of our progress is not whether we add more
to the abundance of those who have much;
it is whether we provide enough for those
who have little.
Franklin D. Roosevelt

Digital Universe

The digital age
brought a bounty of things
to the everyday man and woman.
But as it did, it killed many jobs,
while enriching entrepreneurs and inventors.
There's nothing wrong with benefitting creators,
but many, an everyday woman and man,
must now fend for their lives
as best they can.
Should this trend thus continue,
without training due,
many more will succumb,
digitized out of work
by computers and capital,
to a life without worth,
and the gains of it all
going just to a few.

The goal of the future is full unemployment,
so we can play.
Arthur C. Clarke

Defensive-Aggressive 2

There are people whose self is poorly grown,
they treat every input with mistrust and a frown.
Thus they feel the need to defend
most everything they are faced with to no end.
But it's oft not enough to simply defend,
it is done with aggression –
even worse a bent.
Something happened to them,
likely early in life,
when feelings of betrayal
and a lack of respect
later prevented them to thrive.
This behavior, deeply ingrained,
is hard to change,
it's beyond their awareness,
and without deep searching
forever entrenched.

Remember, no one can make you feel inferior
without your consent.
Eleanor Roosevelt

Vulnerable

Years past when I still traveled a lot,
I happened to land in Denver,
at the old Stapelton port.
Walking down an aisle,
I was suddenly overcome
out of the blue,
by the powerful feeling
of how vulnerable I am.
I did not feel threatened,
did not want it to abate.
Instead I rejoiced
in this wonderful state.

Experience is not what happens to you.
It is what you do with what happens to you.
Aldous Huxley

Wind

I love to listen to the sound
the wind makes traveling through the crowns
of trees, as it has done forever,
across the forests of the world.
Knut Hamsun heard the forests singing.
I hear it, too.
It swells and wanes.
Eternity sings in this sound
that nowhere else is to be found.

How do I know what I think
till I have written it down.
Oswald Veblen

So what!

Once we have reached the age
of five years and three score,
there isn't much
that counts any more.
We now can let go
of most we once treasured,
and the things against which we were weighed and measured.
Mostly we are now free to do as we please,
and should that not suit some,
against reason and rhyme,
we've arrived at the point
when we are, behold,
for better or worse,
like a well-aged, good wine.

Age is strictly a case of mind over matter.
If you don't mind it doesn't matter
Jack Benny

Orthography

Americans, why do you mangle your language?
Why don't you learn better to spell?
Who knows the different uses of every and each,
or the different meanings of beech and beach?
And which, phenomena or phenomenon,
is the singular or the plural?
Is excetera really spelled with an x or a t
or, maybe, even without one?
Between compliment and complement
there is confusion,
and, too, between allusion and illusion.
Then, not to forget that what is meant
is different between imminent and eminent.
And so it goes,
it is a shame.
If there's no change folks,
it will just stay the same.

It is impossible to speak in such a way
that you cannot be misunderstood.
Karl Popper

Confabulation

What we observe and then record,
is often not quite what was there.
We fill the gaps of what we noticed,
adjust facts to what ought to be.
When later we retrieve the story,
we add a few thing which, maybe,
we thought we saw
from our fickle memory.
Alas it was never there to see.
And when we now consider
that we do live by memory,
we ought to ask:
Is this the truth?
Are these the facts?
To what extent is this a tale
or just some made-up history?

Oft, in the stilly night,
ere slumber's chain has bound me,
fond memory brings the light
of other days around me.
Thomas·Moore (1779-1852)

Flight

I crossed the Atlantic in business class;
on a Triple-7 was my flight.
Had champagne, all kinds of goodies, salad, a filet mignon,
and finished it with a sundae to boot.
Yet for more such pleasures I'd have not given a hoot.
There was one thing which would have made the setting just right:
I'd have loved sitting next to me
the fellows who made this all possible:
Orville and Wilbur Wright.

Imagination is more important than knowledge.
Knowledge is limited.
Imagination encircles the world.
Albert Einstein

The Old Country

When I bade my farewell
to my country of birth,
I found it prosperous, well, organized,
her people traveling the Earth.
Yet I couldn't help thinking
that her history's depth
and her narrow streets
did impart on her people,
as educated they are,
a perspective confined
by her history's depth
and her narrow streets.

Don't assume that a species is intelligent
because it produces intelligent individuals.
Jack McDevitt

Eyes

Peoples' demeanor, their diction, their talk,
their scent, their dress,
and how they walk
all play a role
to tell the observer
what they are about.
But the deepest insight he can gain
is through the fact that –
provided they are so possessed –
their eyes are the windows to their soul.

If you do not understand my words,
you will not understand my silence.
Unknown

Insecurity

It takes hold early on,
when we are still young,
barely out of diapers
it's already strong,
never leaving, and festering
no matter what's to come.
Some people succumb,
stay with that role.
Others compensate
with a need for control.

I have never let my schooling interfere with my education.

Marl Twain

Proselytizing

There are these people
of various persuasions
who canvass homes
to promote their wares.
While it is their right
to sell their beliefs,
I quickly check them with my dare
by telling them
that it is the wrong house,
or that they should save their promotion
for a better man.
But sometimes I wonder about my aim,
or rather my writing's content, intent,
and if I'm not doing the very same.

Judge a man by his questions,
not by his answers.
Voltaire

Sun

There, just over the horizon,
hung the sun,
a fiery ball,
as large and sharply defined
and as glorious
as I've ever seen.
Driving, I was heading into it.
I wish
it could have so been.
Alas, as it was,
my goal had to be
the Frankfurt airport
to return to my home,
the U.S. of A.

I hold it to be the inalienable right of anybody
to go to hell in his own way.
Robert Frost

Food

Often, when leftovers are to be eaten,
a mishmash of various foods,
not necessarily aesthetically pleasing
but still nourishing,
I have remarked
how appreciated they would be
by people held captive,
poorly nourished,
in camps of internment, concentration, and as refugees.
As long as food tastes
and does me well,
I will never complain,
for it is better
than to live in hell.

Despair makes victims sometimes victors.
Edward George Bulwer-Lytton

Structure

Some people have it,
others don't.
Some have too much,
others fall short.
If it's too rigid,
it's confining,
and failing that,
it needs defining.
A happy medium sets things right,
for wellness and comfort,
as it might.

Habits in writing, as in life,
are only useful if they are broken
as soon as they cease to be advantageous.
William Somerset Maugham

Coherence 2

With societies becoming wealthier,
better organized and secure,
religion and faith
lose some of their lure.
It is only when misery stalks man
that religion is foremost on his mind.
But what of societies without a faith?
What will make them cohere,
what will take its place?
Can a culture, a society, function without,
can it keep going on,
when everyone's running hither and yon?

Whosoever would be a man
must be a nonconformist.
Ralph Waldo Emerson

Perfectionism

There is no perfection,
only striving for it.
The world is too complex
for us to succeed.
But we must keep on trying
to satisfy this need,
to improve our lives,
against what Nature
throws at us,
which we can never beat.
Perfectionism ought not be pursued.
It is a dead end
and does us no good.

Talk sense to a fool
and he calls you foolish.
Euripides

To Live

It is our fate
           to make decisions.
Then to live
           the decisions –
for better or worse.

New opinions are always suspect,
and usually opposed, without any other reason,
but because they are not already common.
John Locke

Living Together

Humankind has managed,
in the course of time,
to assemble ever greater groups.
And as required by time and place
established societies by various ways and means.
There were chiefs and priests,
and tyrants and kings,
then, at last, the vote for everyone,
of all things.
About this Winston Churchill supposedly said:
"Democracy is the worst form of government,
except for all others that have been tried."
But two thousand five hundred years ago,
Plato worried already that
"The masses were moved by emotion rather than reason,
and by short-term interest,
rather than long-term wisdom,
that citizens would live from day to day,
indulging in the pleasure of the moment."
So what could mankind come up with yet,
to have us function at our very best?

The only thing necessary
for the triumph of evil,
is for good men to do nothing.
Edmund Burke

Aging

is said to be not for sissies,
but darn it,
it isn't fun.
Observing the mental and physical functions slipping
on the way to this final run!
But there is no other way
than to grit your teeth
and keep doing whatever you can.
And once that works no longer
then it's time for good-bye
and to leave the world
for the next generation,
a younger fry.

Death is more universal than life;
everyone dies
but not everyone lives.
Sachs

I don't care!

So often said,
so rarely meant.
Why not reserve it for such situations
that truly call for it to mention?
Why not be careful
with the language,
and use the terms that truly fit,
and thus reserve
"I do not care"
for situations appropriate and rare.

What do you want a meaning for?
Life is a desire, not a meaning.
Charles Spencer Chaplin

Bird Feeder

There, on the deck, is a feeder suspended
right outside the window where we often sit.
House finches are most plentiful,
but many other species come,
and we are happy to count them all.
There are towhees, regular, brown, and Albert,
titmice and chickadees we hail,
sparrows, goldfinches, grosbeaks, and doves,
and even, at times, a daring quail.
A scrubby bluejay will chase others away,
and the visit of a flicker keeps little birds at bay.
Minor goldfinches come also to feed,
but phainopeplas, bushtits, ravens, and hawks,
needing different food will spurn our seeds.
Woodpeckers appear as the season permits,
the pigmies cavort while they catch a bite.
In spring the beautiful lazuli buntings,
northward headed, do come through.
On rare but exciting occasions,
when, at a loss of what we've seen,
we must get our bird book
to learn what kind of bird it has been.
It's a pleasure to observe all this life,
as when young finches beg for food,
or a male feeds a morsel to his mate, his wife.

I don't watch television, I think it destroys the art of talking about
oneself.
Stephen Fry

Radiant

Young woman,
still in the blush of youth,
in the glow of first love,
radiant she is.

Those who know do not speak;
those who speak do not know.
Tao Te Ching

Other Life

We scour space for other life.
Are we afraid to be alone?
Alone in a universe as thinking beings,
unable to talk to someone else – someone?
If only we could find some primitive life,
that would tell us it is possible,
whether of different DNA or not,
to confirm that we aren't an accidental lot.
There's plenty of life
on the planet we dwell,
but none is truly able to ask and to tell.
And, come to think of it,
we don't treat that life very well.
Plenty of planets have been found,
but the answer's still out
if life there abounds,
and if so, is it complex or simple,
and the question remains:
Are we one of many,
or are we single?

The important thing
is not to stop questioning.
Albert Einstein

Taste

No, not good taste for art and decor,
but rather the taste for food and drink.
To satisfy and peruse this craving
is much more basic, the way I think.
There are people who carry eating much too far,
they love to snack and eat the wrong foods.
Others delight in consuming too much
of sugary sodas and harmful booze.
I grew up with the general adage
of eating, drinking, and doing things
"moderately but regularly,"
however, also the dazzling one saying:
"Stupid folks eat,
but intelligent ones guzzle."

Freedom is not worth having
if it does not include the freedom to make mistakes.
Always.
Mahatma Gandhi

Drought

The earth is thirsting,
the soil lifeless and dry.
Dust devils rise and twirl in the wind.
The draught persists,
for how long will it last?
Twenty years it is now,
but we've learned from studies
there were periods much longer,
centuries long,
in the distant past.
Cultures perished,
their people, too.
Some moved, disappeared,
nothing more of them heard.
Water, water,
is what we need!
Yet this hasn't sunk in in many circles
which are still pursuing
exploitation and greed.

Those who fail to learn from history
are doomed to repeat it.
Socrates

Emotion

powers our lives,
unchecked by reason,
leads to quarrel and strife.
It's been our task
since time immemorial
to channel this given
that we may prosper and rise.
When reason fails us,
and emotion persists,
rest assured
our lives will suffer from it.

The wise know too well their weakness to assume infallibility;
and he who knows most, knows best how little he knows.
Thomas Jefferson, Writings

Reason

oft in short supply!
We think we use it
day by day.
But were it so,
we'd do much better,
and in America not kill each other!
For all these murders,
now every week,
are perpetrated from affect,
by the mentally troubled and impaired,
and extremist positions,
sick and defect.
When will the people finally learn
that only rational weapons control
will end this carnage,
while still leaving room for arms to bear?

The ultimate measure of man
is not where he stands in moments of comfort,
but where he stands at times of challenge and controversy.
Martin Luther King, Jr.

Complexity

Most issues we deal with
are simple and plain.
At least that's what folks
assume and maintain.
We quickly confirm
from ideology and belief
what we like to hear
and hold oh so dear.
We would find relief
to step back and hold on,
to probe the complexity,
usually more profound
than our knowledge allows
to judge and propound.
We should be more careful
with the subjects we're facing
and explore them more deeply
before seemingly to explain them.

Any fool can criticize, condemn, and complain,
and most fools do.
Benjamin Franklin

Hide

but not seek
is the ideologist's curse
who's stuck in belief.
Nothing can give!
He's fearful
of losing his bearing in life,
should he venture forth
and apply his intellect
to explore what's the issue,
what life's all about.
How harrowing to think
what all may be lurking
once he looks past belief:
The insecurity, the threats,
he then needs to deal with.
It is thus a comfort,
a featherbed soft,
to stick with belief
and not to explore.

Whenever a theory appears to you as the only possible one,
take this as a sign that you have neither understood the theory
nor the problem which is was intended to solve.
Karl Popper

Departure

There comes a time
in the life of a man,
when he knows
that whatever he could do
has now been done.
Most people aren't aware of that time,
they just hang on
to wait for the chime.
Furthermore, most are afraid
of what's lying in wait,
hell or nothingness,
maybe heaven as bait?
But the greatest fear
for most of them is,
that their meager consciousness
will be the victim
of nothingness.

It is desirable for a man to be blotted out at his proper time.
For as nature has marked the bounds of everything else, so
she has marked the bounds of life.
Moreover, old age is the final scene, as it were, in life's drama,
from which we ought to escape when it grows wearisome and,
certainly, when we have had our fill.
Cicero

Incomplete

The poems I write,
with their subjects addressed,
are never complete,
I must confess.
They are meant to be brief,
fingers put on the pulse,
an invitation to contemplate
what else there may be.
There's lots to think,
to weigh and to probe.
Life is too complex
for a simple poem.
One can only hint and allude
and hope for another
to pursue the thought
he was imbued.

If you want to have good ideas
you must have many ideas.
Linus Pauling

Dissociation

We live at a time of dissociation,
of failing mores, and worse.
Individuals murder for pathological reasons,
or for no reason at all, just to simply kill.
Others, their far out mindsets compelling,
shoot up policemen to send them to heaven or to hell.
Then there are some,
who point lasers at planes,
a potential disaster,
while they think playing games.
And what about those
who are running red lights,
or texting while driving,
killing others, they might.
Why rage in an aircraft and rage on the road?
What is it meaning, what does it connote?
It's society's fabric that is falling apart.
There is no coherence in the direction we sail.
Were it only that people would truly see
that together we rise,
or together we fail.

There is no reality except the one contained in us.
That is why so many people live such an unreal life.
They take the images outside of them for reality
and never allow the world within to assert itself.
Hermann Hesse

Lagoon

Years past,
when I first snorkeled Moorea's lagoon,
I marveled at its colorful life
of corals, fishes, and snails.
And there were other creatures galore,
I then barely knew,
some of which nowadays my memory fails.
But I recall the moray eel,
that faced me from its hiding hole,
its teeth bared but no threat to me.
There were the tiny nips on my body,
on me, the giant invader,
from tiny fishes defending their territory.
Schools of different-size small fishes
patrolled the lapping waves at shore.
Startled, I faced a poisonous lion fish
in shallow waters, barely an arm's length afar.
There had been occasions in my life when
paddling back was the situation's call,
but, rest assured,
this retreat was the swiftest of all.

Do not be too timid and squeamish about your actions.
All life is an experiment.
Ralph Waldo Emerson

Mind Dance

There's never peace
from the dance of thoughts
that rise from the depth of mind.
It may be about food,
or sex, a memory, a sight,
a wish, a decision,
a solution, it might.
Synapses keep firing without rest.
Meditation may help,
but is difficult at best.
What are we to make of this restless prance?
What is its purpose
in life's dance?

Man is fed with fables through life,
and leaves it in the belief he knows something of what is
passing,
when in truth he has known nothing but
what has passed under his own eye.
Thomas Jefferson
Letter to Thomas Cooper

Stop over

There is this couple,
well up in age.
They love it,
when driving by,
I stop.
They pull up some chairs,
we trade some news,
we banter
and share some laughs.
It doesn't seem much,
but when I soon leave them,
I feel enriched.

When you have nothing to say,
say nothing.
Charles Caleb Colto

Mistakes

We are born a blank slate
when we enter life.
We then obtain knowledge
in joy and in strife.
Often it is a drudge to learn,
but some gain the wisdom
to buckle down,
to succeed in acquiring
for what we yearn.
But it is odd to observe
how some people react
to a gentle reminder
that they made a mistake,
when it would simply help them
not to make it again.

There is a deep and pervasive spirit in our species,
which would far rather pursue the emotional phantoms of the
moment
than survive.
Jack McDevitt

Risk

So many kinds of risks there are,
to tackle them requires daring,
leaving the trampled paths behind.
There are those who are driven
by the challenges of life,
while others, afraid,
will never strive.
Different people apply different measures.
What is risk to one,
is another one's pleasure.
Everyone daring must weigh its risk.
Some do it with knowledge,
many are foolhardy,
while others persevere and persist.
If you do not dare,
you are sure not to fail,
but this makes for a life
certainly safe but stale.

Courage is not the absence of fear,
but rather the judgment that something else
is more important than fear.
Ambrose Redmoon

Affect

Affect, emotion, power our lives,
cognition, rationality, control these drives.
Were it not so,
we'd still be grubbing,
in "Nature, red in tooth and claw."
Evolve we did,
beyond other creatures,
with our most precious acquisition,
the ability to reason.
Yet we have still a way to go,
to find the best possible ratio between the two.
For without emotion
we are nothing.
And without reason even less.

Science unleavened by the human heart
and the human spirit is sterile,
cold and self-absorbed.
Gregory A. Petsko

Curiosity

is not restricted just to cats.
It's different from nosiness.
Some people are propelled by either,
while many others have it less.
Then there are some
who ask and ask,
yet do not integrate the information.
It goes in, then and out the other ear,
making for poor curiosity.
True curiosity is mind-enriching.
It broadens knowledge,
is true learning.

He who asks is a fool for five minutes,
but he who does not ask
remains a fool forever.
Chinese proverb

Globalization 2

Yes, here we go again,
kicking and screaming we are headed this way,
whether we want it truly or not.
A path we are on for thousands of years,
of which few are aware,
or give a hoot getting there.
Our path is toward ever greater societies,
a Darwinian "game,"
which we may win,
maybe not.

In a Darwinian universe,
safety is an illusion.
Jack McDevitt

Attitude

Life is a game
we set out to win.
Some never try,
never finding their way.
Most putter along,
do not give it a shot,
react to events,
instead of casting their lot.
If we set our mind,
if we tell it: "We can,"
things fall into place
since we act more assured,
make fewer mistakes.
What it takes, what we need,
is the will to succeed,
and, at times,
a helping hand,
Fortuna's deed.

I hear and I forget.
I see and I believe.
I do and I understand.
Confucius

Winning and Losing

When a game is played,
like the World Cup in soccer,
there usually is a winner and loser.
Should not the victor's delight in success,
call for awareness of the other's loss?
Should not the winners partake in the sorrow,
for today's win
may be their loss in the 'morrow.

An eye for an eye
leaves the world blind.
Mahatma Gandhi

Wisdom

My poetic friend of eighty-eight years,
she, in Germany, I here in the States.
We know each other through e-mail and such.
I recently visited her to stay in touch.
She sent me today a most beautiful poem
from a young German poetess,
who, by the name of Maria Heinrich, is known.
I think she would love to be honored
and not mind my translation, when its German I borrow:

"Ich fühle mich,
als könnte ich
Bäume ausreisen.
Also kleine Bäume.
Vielleicht Bambus.
Oder Blumen.
Na gut, Gras.
Gras geht."

Now, here it goes,
I hope I do right:

"I feel as if
I could pull up trees.
Little ones then.
Maybe bamboo.

Or flowers.
Ah well, grass.
Grass would work."

Poetry is vocal painting.
Simonides of Ceos

Elegy

My friend Annemarie,
I mentioned before,
sent me her poem,
her comment to Maria Heinrich's lore.
It's first in German,
then followed in English,
I did translate it simply,
without embellish:

"Meine Erfahrung:
Zuweilen
wache ich auf
mit großem Elan
plane tausend Dinge
schweren Gewichts
den Tag am Ende
zu beschließen
oh weh
mit Nichts."

"My Experience:
At times
I awake
with great vigor,
plan a thousand things,
solid of nature,

then close the day,
oh dear,
with nothing."

Be wiser than other people,
if you can,
but do not tell them so.
Lord Chesterfield

Black

I once took a black friend to a Sedona resort.
After lunch we hiked Boynton canyon,
where I'd been thrice before.
An avid hiker, Sajo quickly took off,
while I soon decided I had had enough.
I ambled back, then sat on a rock,
when a trio of young graces,
Caucasians were they,
passed by, stopped, and checked if I was okay.
I confirmed my status,
added that I waited for my friend,
to which they commented
that back where they'd come from,
they hadn't met a man.
I said: "He is black,"
to which "Oh" they went,
"Yes he did pass us,
said hi, nothing else."
At the trailhead we caught up with them
getting ready to leave.
So, Sajo and I, a quick study we did,
about who was the prettiest of the three.

All things, even virtue,
are best in moderation.
Garth Urquhart by Jack McDevitt

Displacement

Years past, in Chicago-town,
an Indian restaurant was our favorite haunt.
Occasionally, the owner, no cook,
an Indian native, a political scientist of note,
did join us after dinner
to discuss the world.
At one time he recalled,
when a child still in India,
his mom's admonition:
"Always empty your plate!
For the poor children in Mexico
– remember – have little to eat."

Sweet is the remembrance of troubles
when you are in safety.
Euripides

Prejudice

I once had a friend,
Soon was his name.
I met him in Paris,
from Singapore he came.
We learned French together,
and painted the town.
He told of his family
and the troubles he'd known.
His sister, too, had studied in Britain,
where she'd fallen in love with a Holland man.
She wanted to marry him,
told her Chinese parents
at their Singapore home,
who opposed it violently,
disinherited her, when,
after all, she married her man.
Her parents' objection against her marriage was
that a Caucasian ranked below,
her Chinese status.

Only actions give life strength;
only moderation gives life a charm.
Jean Paul Richter

Hypocrisy

Another friend of my early years,
an engineer, who studied in England,
from Calcutta he was.
Milton Surajit Kumar Guha Thakurta
was his name.
Black as an African,
but with features more slender.
He told me of his mother's admonition
when he left India for Britain.
"Boy," she said,
"I know you are leaving,
likely never to come back.
Somewhere you'll find a wife.
Let her be white or yellow,
but never black!"

Ah! Vanitas vanitatum!
Which of us is happy in this world?
Which of us has his desire, or,
having it, is satisfied.
William Makepeace Thackeray

African-American

There's another friend of 22 years.
I was his best man.
I sometimes call him
my African-American friend.
Born of Italian parents in Tunis, Tunisia,
an American now,
but being from Africa,
he's thus African-American,
a truly multi-ethnic and multi-national man.

There is only one step from the sublime
to the ridiculous.
Napoleon I

Smiles

Is it tears that make us human?
Or the expression of disgust?
Is it fear or is it laughter,
is it shock or is it guile?
Of the above
and more manifestations,
oddly,
some people are hard-pressed to convey,
the most human-to-human sentiment,
the giving of a gentle smile.

Life is a mirror.
If you frown at it, it frowns back.
If you smile,
it returns the greeting.
William Makepeace Thackeray

Sighting

The other day, midmorning it was,
I happened to look into our backyard.
And, lo and behold,
through the bushes strolled
a tawny, black-spotted cat.
About twice the size of a housecat she was,
trailed by two housecat-size kittens.
All three had tails, no tufted ears.
They were not bobcats nor lynxes.
They took their time to amble along,
while I, not of the smart-phone generation,
was not prepared to take a picture,
and so could only go by my observation.
I checked and checked,
and had to conclude,
I spotted, how rare the sighting would be,
a mother with two kits,
three Arizona ocelots.

Enjoy the little things in life,
for one day you'll look back
and realize they were big things.
Kurt Vonnegut

Educated

Oh, it would be so nice
to read Latin and Greek,
play an instrument, do calculus,
deal with quantum mechanics,
paint pictures, know history.
Alas, it's not given
to a simple man.
Wish, he can,
dabble a bit in all,
but that does not make him
a Renaissance man.

The lack of a grave matters little.
Virgil, Aeneid, II

Transients

No, not the transients
who move from place to place.
I mean us all,
mankind, the race.
We are all transients
all life, that is.
If that weren't the case
the planet we live on
would burst at the seams.
But there's more than mere space,
for, when we've had our run,
have had our fill,
it's time to make room
for the generations to come.

The mystery of human existence
lies not in just staying alive,
but in finding something to live for.
Fyodor Mikhailovich Dostoyevsky

Steadfast

To some people it is given
to be steadfast and certain.
Their lives, while not like clockwork,
proceed at a pace.
They don't veer from their paths,
don't cause any upsets,
held in check by their upbringing and creeds.
Their lives, straight as arrows,
are patterned, indeed.
But how impoverished would be the arts of Man,
if all lived such balanced lives?
Through the ages and cultures,
there would have been no materials
for dramas, and tragedies,
for pictures and myths,
and none for great novels, as well.

It is by going down into the abyss
that we recover the treasures of life.
Where you stumble,
there lies your treasure.
Joseph Campbell

Victimhood

Louis Zamperini was a simple man,
troubled from youth to adulthood.
An airman he became in World War Two,
then crashed into the Pacific,
where he was "rescued" by Japanese,
then beaten and starved,
also tortured.
He hated his tormentors
for years to come,
until able to let go of his hate.
There came the day,
when he decided to say:
"I forgive you."
He thus found redemption and dignity,
and succeeded to set himself free.

Never was anything great achieved
without danger.
Niccolo Machiavelli

Balloon

To what little we knew,
we have added a lot.
And the knowledge we've added
is like a balloon.
Inflating it enlarges its volume,
however its surface, too.
And it's the surface that counts,
not the content within.
So the more we inflate this growing balloon,
the more we add to the great unknown.
Thus the harder we blow,
the less we know.

It is one of man's curious idiosyncrasies
to create difficulties
for the pleasure of resolving them.
Joseph de Maistre

Marvel

Smiling usually means showing our teeth.
But millions of years past
this was an expression of fear, of submission,
or, for that matter, of aggression.
The marvel is how it changed over time,
what, in different cultures, it means.
In the West it conveys:
"I like what you said,"
or a tease, a precursor to laughter.
Where the setting is safe, we can even exchange
a smile with a passing stranger.
But beware, dear reader, when you travel abroad,
there are other meanings galore.
Not every culture sees smiling as positive.
No, some find it negative, more.
Others smile when confused or angry,
some when embarrassed or sad, others are suspicious of it,
and some use it to cover emotional pain.
A few reserve it for family and friends.
Most people find too much smiling dishonest and shallow.
But I cannot help to feel delight,
when a woman passes me on the street
and says "Hello" with a pretty smile . . .

perhaps she feels she can be so bold,
because I'm seventy-seven years old.

Do not be too squeamish about your actions. All life is an
experiment.
Ralph Waldo Emerson

Sorrow

All's said below!

There is nothing more tragic in life
than the utter impossibility of changing
what you have done.
John Galsworthy

Doves

There is a neighbor who also feeds birds,
but doesn't like doves to come.
For they gobble and gobble,
depleting her larder,
leaving less for others
by the time they are done.
But when I watch doves
settle on our feeder,
there's something I oft' remember well:
These are the words of my mother,
now gone forty years:
"They are also God's creatures."
It still rings a bell.

As was his language so was his life.
Lucius Annaeus Seneca

Habits

There are all kinds of habits,
but what's common to all
is that over time,
they feel utterly normal.
And there's hardly any awareness
of what's being done.
Most are of piddling importance,
but many are destructive,
hurtful to some.
Rulers and ruled,
without noticing it,
may slide toward the abyss,
wherein the worst of habits,
paranoia, is.

People seem to be hardwired to get things wrong.
They confuse opinion with fact.
They tend to believe what everyone around them believes,
and they are ready to die for the truth
or whichever version of it
they have clasped to their breast.
Armand Ti
by Jack McDevitt

Coyote

The Navajo call the coyote
"The Trickster."
I can't help but feel a kinship with him.
I love to startle,
think outside the box,
or suddenly switch to a different subject.
I love being mischievous,
pulling a leg.
At times, it's okay
to get on my face some egg.
Or to leave something out,
make the other think,
and to help him along
I may give him a wink ;-)

Life is too important
to be taken seriously.
Oscar Wilde

Sandwich

We must give credit to the Earl of Sandwich,
who, a couple of centuries past,
thought of having some meat
tucked between two slices of bread,
and thus created this once English repast.
Growing up in Germany,
two slices of rye bread
became home to a lonely slice of cheese or meat,
with a little butter enlivening this "treat."
Much later, in Canada,
for the first time I had
an American sandwich,
which of the following was made:
a half bun loaded
with mayo, mustard, pickles, and what not.
Plenty of coldcuts and cheese to follow this lot,
until the other half-bun was at last put on top.
Believe me, it tasted unbelievably good,
All hail to the Earl
who invented this food.

Worthless people live only to eat and drink;
people of worth eat and drink only to live.
Socrates

Adage

I grew up with the adage:
"Whatever you do, do it
moderately, but regularly."
When I came to America,
I learned a different one
which was:
"Do everything in excess."
In both exhortations some truth does rest.
It depends on the situation
which choice is best.

Laws are like sausages.
It is better not to see them being made.
Otto von Bismarck

Commonness

I've often said
I could relate to anyone,
of whatever color or creed,
as long as we can respect each other
and have enough in common
for a peaceful meet.
And along that line
I also maintained –
while giving Love its due –
that, what I most value in life
are Competence and Good Will,
without which we'd find much ill.
And when a friend once asked
if I had to choose between the two,
I responded "I'd choose Good Will."
Surprised at my answer,
he asked why that be so?
To which I told him
that with Good Will I may get Competence,
but with Competence only
Good Will might never grow.

There is no conversation more boring
than the one where everybody agrees.
Michel de Montaigne

Cosmos

There stands this bouquet of flowers.
Cosmos is their name.
Green stems and leaves most graceful
vibrantly reach in all directions,
their purplish blossoms doing the same.
The arrangement reminds me
of the woman I love.
But blossoms wilt
when even well watered they are.
There's a time for all seasons,
and their passage afar.
Will watering my love
keep it from wilting?
Maybe?
Will I find the right moisture?
This flower's meaning:
Peace and tranquility.

When you make a sacrifice in marriage,
you're sacrificing not to each other
but to the unity in a relationship.
Joseph Campbell

Limits

There are limits to what can be proffered to people
by individuals, cities, countries, and states.
Or, should I say:
What ought to be offered
that can truly be delivered in a future day?
But the system we live by
is that those who promise,
when the time comes to deliver,
will no longer hold sway.
So, for short-term gain
and to hold on to power
these promisers chuck responsibility.
There's also the limit
of what we ought to control,
to regulate for the well-being of all.
Too little brings ill,
too much may kill
our very foundations of vigor and will.

An election is coming.
Universal peace is declared,
and the foxes have a sincere interest
in prolonging the lives of the poultry.
George Eliot

Point

What I write on a subject
is never enough.
It's only to make a point.
Most everything is too complex by far
to address in depth,
to give it its due.
But if my point leads the reader to ponder,
and enter the subject more deeply to wonder
how very complex most everything is,
then my intent did not miss
in this peculiar quest for success.

It is one of the most beautiful compensations of this life
that no man can sincerely try to help another
without helping himself.
Ralph Waldo Emerson

Africa

I have been to the deserts,
the Namib, the Sahara.
I've canoed the Zambezi,
crossed the plain of Amboseli.
Ballooned the Mara, chased hippos in that river,
had elephants chasing me in Botswana.
Seen ancient ruins most plentiful,
in Morocco, Libya, and Egypt.
Entered the Valley of Kings and Hatshepsut's temple
with my buddy, the only visitors there.
I have walked the bush in tow of a guide,
his rifle at the ready,
always wondering what the next thicket might hide.
I've seen giraffes, antelopes, crocs,
warthogs and lions galore,
elephants, buffalo, and many more,
seen them by daylight and in the night.
I've met and enjoyed
many people from near and afar.
Believe me, dear reader,
when I hold it dear and say here:
"There's always the call of Africa."

The goal of life
is to make your heartbeat match the beat of the universe,
to match your nature with Nature.
Joseph Campbell

Friend

Whom we call friend
is determined by culture.
And cultures are different, for sure.
Even when seemingly similar per se,
the meaning of terms may subtly vary.
Thus it is with "friend" and the friendship to follow.
Americans readily call someone a "friend,"
met only briefly but thought of well.
As the friendship grows a "good friend" evolves.
Whom Americans call friend
is an "acquaintance" to Germans.
If a friendship develops, they will call him a "friend,"
and believe greater depth theirs have
than American ones.
Like the Germans the Turks have two personal pronouns,
the formal and the familiar one.
I've always wondered whether this duality
the English language does not have,
makes the recognition of a stranger as friend,
just a touch more more difficult in the end.
Loyalty is a Turk's hallmark of friendship.
Once extended it grows and endures.
At least in this respect the two cultures are similar,
so Teutonic in their mores.

Follow your bliss and the universe will open doors
where there were only walls.
Joseph Campbell

Reality Check

From time to time,
we need a reality check,
some people more,
some less.
We can call our sliding
into non-reality
a rut, a habit, a delusion,
a misconception or illusion
which affects individuals and groups.
Entire nations fall victim to it.
But the people needing a check most dearly,
are those in power,
for their "reality"
becomes distorted more clearly.
It is the tyrants
gaining power by force
who become deluded most.
This is why functioning governments,
from time to time,
replace those in power
to weigh un-reality's cost.

It is not the strongest of the species that survive, nor the most
intelligent,
but the ones most responsive to change.
Charles Darwin

Outlook

There are some who see impending doom,
while others see our species bloom.
So, who is right?
The pessimists,
who correctly see
our increasing complexity,
with which we deal only haphazardly.
Then, there are the optimists
who think
that our ever increasing knowledge
will keep us from the looming brink,
make for an ever better life.
I hope they are right,
that our future is bright.
But there is this doubt that with all our strife,
that technology will make for a better life.

For all evils there are two remedies –
time and silence.
Alexandre Dumas

Personality

We enter life with the genes we are given,
the nutrition derived and the toxins' effect
exposed in the mother's womb.
Thereafter we live from what affected us most,
experiences depressing and elevating.
Those that put us on a track
happen in childhood,
then propel us forward, sometimes back.
They are hard to fathom,
still harder to change,
and cover a wide behavioral range.
They give us strength
for what we accomplish.
They make us who we are.
Sometimes a curse,
we cannot escape them.
It can only be said:
For better or worse.

Nothing is permanent in this wicked world –
not even our troubles.
Charles Spencer Chaplin

Vanity

The other day I was asked:
"Are you vain?"
"No, I'm not,"
was my retort.
"I only want to leave a decent impression."
How could I be vain,
when my paternal grandmother,
under whose tutelage I grew up,
kept saying:
"If a bottle of wine
would cost five marks,
and a bucket-full fifty pfennigs,
we would only drink from buckets."
No vanity there!

Philosophy is the art of living.
Plutarch

Driven

There are people motivated and propelled
to fully involve themselves
in whatever activity their biology or experience
pushes and compels.
Oft inaccessible to the conscious mind,
it is their way of engaging the world.
Whether it's climbing the mountain that's there,
jumping from cliffs, or another dare.
Whether it's sex,
succeeding in business,
or being at a sport's apex.
Only people of similar nature,
no matter their different drives,
can understand the force, its power,
that makes them feel alive.
Others, not endowed or cursed in this manner,
will not appreciate the push it imparts.
Hard as they try,
they will not succeed,
their comprehension encumbered
by their missing drive.
There can be no understanding,
believe me,
none!

Life is simply what our feelings do to us.
Honore de Balzac

Resemblance

There are people, the faithful,
who go by their Book.
It is truth revealed,
the very word of God,
doubt is not brooked.
Two groups have this in common,
resembling each other true.
They are Fundamentalist Christians,
and believe it or not,
all Muslims, too!

Life is the art of drawing sufficient conclusions
from insufficient premises.
Samuel Butler

Sequoias

I've walked the growths of sequoias,
along the California coast.
Evergreen, they rise to the heavens,
majestic in their peace, their silence,
yet their stand against fate
is precarious for most.
Some have been felled by lightning,
others by age,
but those now lying on the earth
are nurse logs for new generations
to last for centuries and more.
Giant ferns are covering the ground,
their fronds, a mantle green, abound.
At times, there's a squirrel,
way up high,
rarely a bird's twitter or a cry.
Let's hope these sacred groves will last
for generations yet to come.
Eighty for humans,
while only one for sequoias,
at least for some.

May you live all the days of your life.
Jonathan Swift

Acceptance

We are who we are,
established at birth,
and the first few years.
For better or worse,
we make our lives.
With some insight and pluck
and a bit of luck,
we arrive at old age,
and look back to say
"We didn't do badly."
But it's impossible
to do everyone right,
so it's up to these others
to deal with such blight
and accept what has been,
to see the light,
to forget and remember,
but look forward
to what's yet to come, what might.

The supreme happiness of life is the conviction that we are
loved;
loved for ourselves,
or rather in spite of ourselves.
Victor Hugo

Community

What makes a community?
A unified body of individuals,
a commonwealth?
People of common interest
interacting together,
looking out for themselves
and for each other?
Does not the third line above tells it all?
That such a people
look out for their common wealth,
of whatever nature that be,
material and health.
When this outlook fails,
when people no longer give a damn,
then the end isn't far,
and you'd better run.

The mystery of human existence lies not in just staying alive,
but in finding something to live for.
Fyodor Mikhailovich Dostoyevsky

Geology

I wish my poems were like it,
to last for time immemorial.
Alas, ephemeral they are,
very much like myself.
This is fine by me.
So be it.
Yet I love the striations,
the layers of sandstone,
their hue of colors,
laid and eroded by desert winds
in the Arizona and Utah Red Rock lands.
What's the affinity I feel for these strata
that time and circumstance
add and take away?
Is it a kinship I feel,
although I'm a nothing,
a life lived much shorter
under different sway?

The privilege of a lifetime is being who you are.
Joseph Campbell

Security

What security?
Rest assured,
there's none!
Only vagaries accompany us
on our life's run.
We keep trying
to make our lives secure,
may succeed for awhile,
then think to have made it,
when in fact it was just allure.
Individuals and groups fall victim to it,
even nations, grandiose,
have faced this pit.
The universe isn't made to be danger-free.
There is risk everywhere,
yet we fail to see
from our ephemeral perspective
there can never be
the security we long for
in the present, as well as the future,
which we cannot foresee.

Participate joyfully in the sorrows of the world.
We cannot cure the world of sorrows,
but we can choose to live in joy.
Joseph Campbell

Scent

When it rains in Arizona,
which it rarely does,
the juniper trees exude a scent
so fresh, so delicate, so well,
it's a delight to inhale it, to smell.
The earth then seems to breath in, too,
coming alive with the life-giving water.
For decades the land has been thirsting now.
Will this continue for years,
even decades to come,
as in centuries past it has frequently done?
In summer the monsoons provide plenty of moisture,
but soon, by September they are exhausted, gone.
Water, water, the elixir of life,
with it we prosper,
without it we perish,
we can't stay alive.

In rivers, the water that you touch
is the last of what has passed
and the first of that which comes;
so with present time.
Leonardo da Vinci

Fact

I hold this truth to be self-evident
that a fact is something existing,
a truth, an objective reality,
an occurrence, actuality.
A fact is neither good nor bad,
whatever it is, it simply is.
It's only what we make of it
that gives it meaning:
goodness or evil.
It can be misused or be beneficial.
Misapplied, it can be hurtful,
properly used it can do wonders galore.
But in the end
it remains a fact,
a mere statement
of what has happened before.

The causes of events are ever more interesting
than the events themselves.
Marcus Tullius Cicero

Oneness,

the unity of mind.
Does it exist in the human world,
or are we all one of a kind?
Are we confined in this skull of ours?
Is it a prison we cannot escape?
We don't want to be ants,
nor do termites call,
but I wish, I long
to have it all,
to be able to share what's on my mind,
deeply, intensely,
become one with the other,
to at least, for a while,
be like Spock, his kind.

When you make the sacrifice in marriage,
you're sacrificing not to each other
but to unity in a relationship.
Joseph Campbell

Cats Again

I have two bilingual cats,
sixteen years old,
with lots of smarts.
No matter the language I talk in and tell,
I'm sure they understand me very well.
Alas, as cats do,
they follow their creed,
no matter the language used,
English, German, even Greek.

Wear none of thine own chains,
but keep free, whilst thou art free.
William Penn, *Fruits of Solitude*

Risk 2

In risking something
we court failure.
Not risking something
we fail, too.
Not having tried
we'll never know
the gain we missed
had we pursued
that which was waiting
for us unbeknownst,
had we but dared
to find out how
what we are capable of doing,
which is much more
then we'll ever know.

Never was anything great achieved without danger.
Niccolo Machiavelli

Pyracantha,

how tall you can be
with your berries orange or red
now, in fall, so pleasant to see.
There is a bush, almost a tree,
just outside my window,
at least twelve feet tall it may be.
It draws lizards and birds,
a chipmunk sometimes clambering through,
looking into my window,
as if saying hello.
Late in fall, I've observed before,
waxwing flocks, maybe twenty or more,
descending on it,
devouring the berries,
baring the bush, or is it a tree?

Life is like an onion:
you peel it off one layer at a time,
and sometimes you weep.
Carl Sandburg

Mindsets

Such an innocent word,
However within rests palm leaf or sword.
We all have mindsets to live by.
Some people by one live all their life,
others adopt different ones to try.
Our adopted mindsets
appear as our reality,
no matter how far
from what the majority of humans
may think they are.
A mindset, innocent, may be benign,
another result in a lot of pain.
There is a gradation, a ladder effect,
that reaches the ultimate
in a Hitler, a Gadhafi, an Assad,
and the other oh so sorry lot.
This is why, from time to time,
we all need a reality check
to make certain our cards
are properly stacked.

We don't see things as they are;
we see things as we are.
The Talmud

Wonder

In nineteen-forty-three
the worst of The War was yet to come.
Just six years old,
we vacationed in Bavarian lands.
I marveled at the Alpenglow,
and the peaceful lake we stayed by below.
Its water, so clear, that way down one could see,
the varied life abounding there,
a first time this, it was for me.
From a tiny dock, with the help of a sieve,
crayfish, snails, and even some fish,
were we able to retrieve.
Ten years later, on my first solo trip,
I ventured back to recapture the magic
I once had found there.
Alas, it was gone.
The lake was bare.
There's a first time for everything.
Rarely can we experience the wonder
of the first time, once more.

Life begins on the other side of despair.
Jean Paul Sartre

Friends

When trouble strikes,
severe at times,
as is bound to happen,
some friends are there,
while others are not
or need to beware.
Some cannot deal with the subject at hand,
others live in a different land.
Some react as if the Earth were flat,
dropping off its edge,
rarely to be heard from again.
Some friends are steady, as they go,
new ones appear one barely did know.
And others, from whom one heard little before,
one now hears concern,
gets attention much more.
Ah, such is life,
but what does it prove?
Just that people are different
not deserving reproof.

Life is a tragedy for those who feel
and a comedy for those who think.
Jean de La Bruyere

145

Hugs

For a couple of days I joined the group,
translator for eight German visitors
I hadn't met before.
I suggested we use first names
and the German "du,"
something friendlier than the English "you."
They were affiliates of Prescott's sister city, Zeitz,
whose mayor was along for the umpteenth time.
We went to museums and shopped quite a bit.
The Indian Powwow and Whiskey Row they enjoyed,
all, sure were a hit.
We had fun, guzzled beer, and
at the Mayor's reception poked fun here and there.
Then, when we said our good-byes in downtown Prescott,
there, on a sidewalk, on the spot,
supposedly stiff and formal Germans amazed me.
I could believe it not.
One after the other they gave me a hug.
It was the best Thank You
I ever got.

You will never be happy if you continue to search
for what happiness consists of.
You will never live if you are looking for the meaning of life.
Albert Camus

The Noise

In the stillness of night,
and in a restful day,
there is a noise
that keeps thumping away.
It sounds like the pistons
that drive a steamship.
For as long as there's fuel
for the fires to leap,
it propels the ship
against current and fate.
And come the day
when the fire burns down,
the ship runs aground,
the pumping heart
stops its sound.

The goal of life
is to make your heartbeat match the beat of the universe,
to match your nature with Nature.
Joseph Campbell

Shadow

A shadow hangs over everyone.
Few are alive for whom it does not.
Some, in its darkness, walk lifelong.
Others decide to look for the sun.
Some do this early,
some do it late.
Those who do not
never change their fate.

We never live;
we are always in the expectation of living.
Voltaire

Deliberate

Hasty or deliberate,
the latter appeals in a cat.
Dogs love to sniff, crave attention, and pounce,
which is worth to me, shucks,
less than an ounce.
I don't care to be licked
and slobbered all over
by any, a Max, a Buster, or Rover.
But if a cat should lick me
most gentle and tender,
it's an honor
no dog can ever render.

That which costs little
is less valued.
Miguel de Cervantes

Northwoods

I canoed many times in northwoods waters,
the Boundary and Quetico lakes.
Once, I set off with four adults and six kids,
four canoes, oodles of backpacks,
one holding twenty-four loaves of bread.
Eleven days we had planned for the trip,
but one hundred degrees-plus did right away hit.
The second day we adults thought to quit,
but to be fair, put the subject to a vote,
and promptly the result was six to four.
We sweated on, then had to mind –
each campsite furnished with a place of rest –
so-called by our friend John's name,
to clearly distinguish, not to confuse the same.
Then, one night – we had two tents –
the better campsite had gone to our friends,
our own on a slightly canted slope,
when in the night a thunderstorm broke.
And the Devil willed that a runnel rushed down,
right into our tent, its entrance exposed,
and at the end formed a lake, lo and behold.
So, for the kids not to drown in the tent,
I poked a hole at the very end.
The water receded, relief was at hand,
no matter that a creek still flowed through the tent.

At last we returned to civilization so dear,
and the delightful taste of an ice-cold beer.

That which yields is not always weak.
Jacqueline Carey

Te Quiero

Am I right?
Is it true?
Am I really sure?
Can that which I seek
truly be found,
or is it just a lure
that keeps me suspended
to try forever, of course, in vain,
to find that which cannot be found,
only pain?
But I love the pursuit,
the horizon is close,
to continue the search,
for there must be one.

Find a place inside
where there's joy,
and the joy will burn out the pain.
Joseph Campbell

Birthday

Today is my birthday,
my seventy-eighth.
I marvel how far I got
in all the years that went by,
wherein many people crossed my path.
I wonder what happened to this varied lot?
Some stayed for a time,
others' presence was brief,
but what of the many who,
much too early, left this earthly fief?
Was I just lucky? Did I do something right,
that I now linger in these years of twilight?
If health serves me well,
and my will does too,
there may yet be years for plenty to do.

A life spent making mistakes is not only more honorable,
but more useful than a life spent doing nothing.
George Bernard Shaw

Labor

Much of my work through the past forty years
dealt with computers and mental affairs.
Yet I always liked to grub in the dirt,
to compensate for the mental efforts,
and make up for them by this physical part.
So I built with my hands,
cleared overgrown yards,
erected stone walls,
built drainage swales and flagstone stairs.
I have always held that good work ennobles,
applying to the Indian Outcasts as well.
Untouchables they may be,
cleaning privies all day,
but a job well done
demands respect,
as surely as any other may.

The shoe that fits one person pinches another;
there is no recipe for living that suits all cases.
Carl Gustav Jung

Mentor

I have a nonagenarian friend
whose memory goes back to the twenties.
She tells me stories from her early life
and how conditions were then.
There raged the Recession
when she was barely twelve
and where she grew up was the pits.
But there was this man,
an inventor of sorts,
who took her under his wing.
He instilled in her the worth of her being,
accepted and taught her well.
A mentor in the best of sense,
he was able to propel
this girl, barely into her teens,
to a successful life as well.
Oh, how often I have wished for a mentor in kind.
Alas, none ever materialized, came.
What I regret ever more, however,
was that I was unable do the same.

One of the luckiest things that can happen to you in life is,
I think, to have a happy childhood.
Agatha Christie

155

Tranquility

Whatever happened to this precious state
that we have lost in our world?
Do we need music everywhere,
the loudest sort, the worst of fare?
Is it that noise is covering up
the emptiness contained in Rap?
Is it that people are afraid
lest silence make them think?
Why is it that folks need this racket?
To deaden senses or their lack?
And airport lounges are the worst.
It is a marvel at the best
that people put up with this noise.
By God, give me another choice!
Such as a starlit sky, the heaven's vault,
where peace does dwell
for thoughts to grow.

The masses of mankind are evidently slavish in their tastes,
preferring a life suitable to beasts.
Aristotle

Retribution,

a concept strange.
It holds no power,
is bound to fail.
A reward it may be,
in which case it's okay.
But as punishment, supposed,
it will hound the perpetrator
to the end of the world.
Not aware of it,
he will struggle on,
unable to let go
of what brought it on.

In taking revenge a man is but even with his enemy;
but in passing it over, he is superior,
for it is a prince's part to pardon.
Francis Bacon

Starlight

dimming ever more,
the lights of Man concealing.
With mankind gathering evermore
in cities, their prevailing lights
preventing starry nights' revealing.
To see the glory of the vault of heaven,
we soon must head for deserts, large,
to forests, deep, and oceans, vast.
Or, what an irony it is,
head into space
to see the stars.

For all evils there are two remedies –
time and silence.
Alexandre Dumas

Imponderables

I have been confronted with things that are
imponderable, impossible to weigh.
So I imagined a circle of knowledge
in whose center those items that, by far,
are the most solid, real, and hard.
A table, a cat, a house, a plant,
is touchable, cannot be split, cannot be rent.
Okay, dear reader, bear with me a bit,
I know these apparently solid items
can, with some effort, also be split.
But, the farther I travel the circle's center
outward to its periphery,
the less certain become those items of knowledge
that I try to understand.
There is, for instance, quite a way out,
the function of the human mind.
And just inside the circle's outer ring,
there's quantum mechanics,
which works, but not enough is known about.
Then, when I step outside this ring,
that's where the weird imponderables begin.
I happily decided to let them be,
such as Dark Matter and Dark Energy.
There's also belief in extra-sensory perception,
the Multiverse and String theory.

So I wait until things fall into place
to enter inside the circle's periphery.
Once this has happened there's yet time to ponder
these items to my heart's content.

I am not young enough to know everything.
Oscar Wilde

To Let Be

In the absence of evidence
and the proper interpretation of data,
it is foolish to draw conclusions.

Every religion is true one way or another.
It is true when understood metaphorically.
But when it gets stuck in its own metaphors,
interpreting them as facts,
then you are in trouble.
Joseph Campbell

Writing

There are days of dearth,
no thoughts will jell.
Then, suddenly, if all goes well,
they tumble from the opened mind
demanding: Put us down,
be quick,
before we disappear again.
No matter where one is right then:
They say:
go to it, write till you're done.

Occasions are rare;
and those, who know how to seize upon them,
are rarer.
Henry Wheeler Shaw

Feat

What feat it is to empty mind,
to stop the torrent of thoughts
that pursue us day and night.
What else are dreams
but private myths,
thoughts of the sleeping kind?
Awake, these thoughts keep tumbling forth,
irrational, oft unconnected.
They can be creative or numbing dull,
some so haunting, we continue to mull.
There is meditation to hold this pursuit,
to find peace for a while,
to subdue our thoughts,
tone them down, make them mute.

Myths are public dreams,
dreams are private myths.
Joseph Campbell

Novae

and supernovae, creators of life,
which, in their death throes,
their mighty explosions,
somewhere, somewhen
make it possible, provide,
the higher mass elements,
carbon, oxygen, nitrogen, calcium,
potassium and phosphorus,
required for life.
Without them the universe would be empty, void,
nothing to ponder,
give meaning to,
to suffer and to enjoy.
Once that is done
we do what we ought.
Return to the starstuff
from which we were wrought.

What do you want a meaning for?
Life is a desire, not a meaning.
Charles Spencer Chaplin

Sensitivity

is a two-edged sword,
great for plumbing the depths of the world,
her violence, her love, her ignorance,
and whatever else can be felt and heard.
It can be joyful, exhilarating,
what all there is,
yet it comes at a price:
Its oft painful experience.

Find a place inside where there's joy,
and the joy will burn out the pain.
Joseph Campbell

Beauty

How to describe it, so manifold?
It all depends on who beholds.
A rising sun on an ocean vast,
an African sunset made hazy by dust?
A woman's smile, lit from inside,
The Alhambra illuminated by moonlight?
The vault of heaven, everlast?
A Japanese dish, a delightful repast?
An Alpine valley bathed in light,
the Rocky Mountains, stark and bright?
Desert dunes to the far horizon,
a forest glade, lit by the sun?
A picture painted to stir the soul?
The Ode to Joy, so powerful?
I could go on and on and on!

The more we live by our intellect,
the less we understand the meaning of life.
Lev Nikolaevich Tolstoy

Email,

oh, so ephemeral,
all deleted, nothing kept.
Few care these days about their spelling.
Texting is the worst of it.
How I pity future writers,
authors of biographies.
Where, oh where will they find letters,
records for posterity?
And the electronic storage,
fade it will that which is kept.
And of material we're recording
I wonder what stays worthwhile still?
Love, once true and without fail,
declared on paper, taking time,
is it now ephemeral as email?

Nothing is permanent in this wicked world –
not even our troubles.
Charles Spencer Chaplin

Gnarled

Branches and roots
gnarled by climate and fate,
oh, what character some have acquired.
Like faces of women and men,
when you see them you know, you ken.
What all they have seen,
suffered through, understood,
that their faces gained character,
the likeness of wood?

Life is like an onion:
you peel it off one layer at a time,
and sometimes you weep.
Carl Sandburg

Hiking

We hiked the trails of Burgundy,
the Alsace and Provence.
The first hike started in Cluny
from where the first Crusade was urged.
Another pilgrim route begins there, too,
one we were loath to cross.
It ends in Compostela, Spain,
at the shrine of Santiago Matamoros.
No, we enjoyed a leisurely walk
through villages, vineyards, and fields,
and evenings indulged in some wine
with a delicious French repast
which we concluded – what delight –
by selecting as dessert,
the most fragrant cheese from the cart.
Goat's milk being its pleasant source,
which, in the course of time and love,
was fashioned by man's art.

In the world there are only two tragedies.
One is getting what one wants,
the other is getting it.
Oscar Wilde

Walk-About

is what young male Aborigines do,
supposedly to find out who they are
and what they are up to.
It does not refer only to those Down Under,
oh no, closer to home,
it also cleaves relations asunder.
Ah, if we only knew who we are,
to overcome our problems,
without pain, without scars.
Amerindians did something similar, akin.
So, if these searches lead to solutions,
there's nothing lost,
if all of us win.

The causes of events are ever more interesting
than the events themselves.
Marcus Tullius Cicero

Lowest Common Denominator

Commercial interests dominant,
making money is the ultimate want.
Thus video games, TV, and such,
are suff'ring from this headlong rush
by catering to the basest tastes.
Well to the bottom heads this race.
It's getting worse, and worse, and worse,
this fare of superstition, violence,
of false beliefs and ignorance.
Where will it end,
if no one cares,
if no one really gives a damn,
to raise and educate the common man
as once by libraries was done?

If you create an act, you create a habit.
If you create a habit, you create a character.
If you create a character,
you create destiny.
William Makepeace Thackeray

Sorrow 1

Life can catch up with you
toward the end of your days,
when you ponder the things you have done.
Good actions took you to where you are now,
but others caused plenty of sorrow.
Immutable these actions are,
good and bad alike.
Time heals some,
but others not,
and carries on
the sorry lot.

Your life is the fruit of your own doing.
You have no one to blame but yourself.
Joseph Campbell

Eternal Life

I just watched a javelina sow
amble across my backyard,
two suckling piglets in tow.
They are born, grow up, procreate, fade away,
and return to the earth,
as all life must die.
It's been said that all life that ever was
would equal the mass of the Earth.
It, too, applies to us humans,
no matter that we don't want our lives to pass.
There's also the question of the mass of souls,
if any weight they have,
thus might weigh down, endanger Heaven.
The best explanation I may present
for Heaven not having collapsed onto Earth,
is
that all too few weighty souls must have made it yet
to this supposedly heavenly place.

If we don't know life,
how can we know death?
Confucius

Sarcasm

I cannot help at times to deride
this well-entrenched human deceit
that we are the crown of creation
with the Earth at our feet.
So, I feel, it's good to stir the pot,
not be subtle or sublime.
The way it looks,
there's a long way to go
for us to improve our lot.
So, let's work on it,
be not overbearing,
and get out of this terrible rut.
And if we are lucky
and get the chance,
we will make it,
given time.

The world is a dangerous place to live,
not because of the people who are evil,
but because of the people
who don't do anything about it.
Albert Einstein

174

Water,

fresh, good, drinkable water
gets ever more scarce to come by.
Seventy percent of Earth is covered by water,
the oceans hold salty ninety-seven of it.
The remaining piddling little bit,
is held in aquifers, rivers and lakes,
or is locked up in glaciers and ice.
If we keep wasting this precious resource
in low-tech agricultural ways,
with lawns in the desert
and the pleasures of golf –
forget not the toxins we discharge –
with humanity still increasing,
and many not having yet a decent source,
well, there's plenty of salty water,
expensive to desalinate,
as a last recourse.

An unfortunate thing about this world is
that the good habits are much easier to give up
than the bad ones.
William Somerset Maugham

Dents

I've driven fifty-three years
without a road accident.
A passive-aggressive driver,
I seem to have known
to do what and when.
Over years, on my driveways,
I produced a few dents,
but they weren't reported,
being extraordinary events.

What we anticipate seldom occurs;
what we least expect generally happens.
Benjamin Disraeli

Hunting and Fishing

I've fished Caribbean waters and Australia's, too,
mind you, not for anything big and ferocious.
Then a little off Nova Scotia and Alaska to boot.
Of course, there were also Canadian lakes.
In Minnesota it showed that I lacked what it takes.
But it was always exciting when a fish took the bait,
then broke the surface,
where I lay in wait.
I went only once to hunt for deer,
but never to a doe nor a buck I got near.
I'm just not a hunter,
more a city boy.
But it was fun to have done it,
that I gave it a try.

When the time comes in which one could,
the time has passed in which one can.
Marie von Ebner-Eschenbach

Cognac

Once, years ago, traveling with Club Med
at their Moorea resort, I went to the bar
to order a couple of drinks.
There approached this wahine, swaying in her pareau,
to check for my want, saying kindly "hello."
I dug up my French and proceeded to say:
"Deux Cognac, ma chère, si'l vous plais."
That very moment a traveling friend
tapped my shoulder and I turned to chat.
When I glanced back how my snifters were coming,
the woman still stood there smiling.
I wondered what caused her to stop in her tracks
and repeated my order:
"Two brandies, deux Cognacs!"
She kept smiling, then busied herself with the job.
I turned back to my friend to finish my talk.
When I again faced my Tahitian hostess,
there she stood smiling, presenting four glasses.
I knew I'd been had, but kept a straight face,
and paid the vixen with what I thought was good grace.
When I then tasted my plentiful lot,
it turned out, the Cognac was real, very good.
The brandy, well, tasted like brandy should.

Do not be too squeamish about your actions.
All life is an experiment.
Ralph Waldo Emerson

Mary Jane

I met her many decades past,
alas, the acquaintance didn't last.
There I sat on a pleasant Sunday morn,
on a bench, with a friend, looking over the land.
I had always thought that telephone poles,
their wires strung through the sky,
messed up the sights, looked ugly as hell.
But suddenly, out of the blue,
these contraptions looked quite swell.
At Sunset Beach we walked the sand,
at times found beautiful shells.
Only fragments they were, tumbled into intriguing shapes,
I collected them for necklaces to make.
There came a time, joined by Mary Jane,
that we found sacks of such beautiful shapes.
When, the following day we looked at the take,
we wondered what had possessed us there.
Mary Jane can be strong,
enhance your sensations,
distort your perspective,
and make you feel good.
But at times she is fickle
and feeling off, she may also be bad,
affecting more than your mood.

It is easier to preach virtue than to practice it.
La Rochefoucauld

Fatum

Destiny, the fate, the doom of everything.
The universe, its suns, its planets,
their seas and mountains
sundered, broken, taken in.
But life, especially, is ephemeral,
yet few, if any animals have any sense of it.
It's left to us,
these semi-conscious beings,
to contemplate the life we're given,
to ponder our grief and joy.
For most, it's but a misery of living,
For few a life of love and giving,
for all too many, if they're lucky,
a mediocre trek to death.
And on that way
we deal with losses, strife, or failing health, and more.
It is no wonder that for many
the only comfort is religion's lore.

Life without the courage for death is slavery.
Lucius Annaeus Seneca

Awareness,

it most precious is,
yet difficult to bring to life,
requiring constant probing, weighing.
To check for dearly held beliefs and patterns,
which, unchecked, distort our actions,
hold us captive forever on.
We can be, oh so unaware of what we do,
repeating poor, hurtful behavior,
carry it on for years and years
and never realize the rotten fruit it bears.
There are the piddling things that do not matter.
But watch some of the careless driving patterns
which tell us that these drivers, sure,
are largely unaware of what they do,
their interactions being very poor.
One could continue on and on,
but you, the reader, can start checking
what all there is that need be done.

Two-thirds of what we see is behind our eyes.
Chinese proverb

Google

The fount of knowledge Google has become
is utterly amazing, a googlish sum.
Mankind's latest gathering of information
to be found in this compendium of Man.
One must be aware
of misinformation there,
but on the whole,
it's a treasure, all told.
But what if this digital wonder should ever fail?
What can take its place,
what will avail?
The Net makes us smarter
and keeps us in touch,
but should it ever shut down,
beware fellow-man,
we'll be out of luck.

Never trust a computer you can't throw out a window.
Steve Wozniak

Taking for Granted

Our familiar world holds true just so far,
but what if it suddenly fails?
Young and old do hold this position
and amble through life
as if nothing will change.
Yet all it takes is to check the record
to show what all may descend on us,
individually or on groups, it does.
There's much yet to happen across the world.
It will strike here and there, not everywhere.
Let's hope this stays true,
we can live with this.
What're a few thousand lives
of the billions we now are?
It's a terrible thought, but that's our fate.
We keep trying to make our lives ever better,
and have succeeded quite well,
but never should we take life for granted,
for not far from this goodness
lurks the occasional hell.

Misery motivates, not utopia.
Karl Marx

Spanish

I'm trying to learn Spanish at seventy-eight,
which, come to think of it,
is a little bit late.
But my French's all but faded,
of little use in America's west.
So, with the Hispanic Reconquista,
to know a little Spanish may be the best,
just to get me around,
exchange a word here and there
with my fellow-immigrants,
some of whom have been earlier here.
But we should all speak English,
or American, for that matter,
if only to keep this nation together.

Piecemeal social engineering resembles physical engineering
in regarding the ends as beyond the province of technology.
Karl Popper

Negligence

For two people
to keep each other company
year after year,
it takes maintenance, refreshment, and good cheer.
If these are not done,
there's a drifting apart.
To recover its spring tide
takes more than art.
It's so easy to fall into a rut or worse.
Neglect takes its toll
and brings on the hearse.

When people get married
because they think it's a long-time love affair,
they'll be divorced very soon,
because love affairs end in disappointment.
But marriage is a recognition of a spiritual identity.
Joseph Campbell

Open House

I grew up in a family with an open house.
A grandmother's grocery store advanced this cause.
People drifted in for a purchase, a chat,
for a hello, a visit, and what not.
It was all so colloquial, informal, a pleasure,
years later I still consider it a treasure.
Located on the banks of the Rhine,
there were skippers who dropped in
to buy their victuals and wine.
Some became friends
while they traveled up and downstream.
A lunch or a meal was frequently seen.
Formality is great and has its place,
but I do enjoy a casual house.

Passionate hatred can give meaning
and purpose to an empty life.
Eric Hoffer

Bougainvillea

boisterous,
your colors yellow, red, or blue,
white and purple, orange, too.
Where I see you life is enhanced,
emboldened, lively,
I'm entranced.

May you live all the days of your life.
Jonathan Swift

Customs

There are plenty of people around the world
who know nothing better than to eat with bare hands.
A few chop their meat just shy of their lips,
some use a spoon into their soups to dip.
Many use chopsticks, or a fork to slip
their food onto a spoon from which they nip.
There are also the Europeans
who firmly use knife and fork
organized as a feeding means.
But the oddest eaters Americans are,
a people otherwise practical,
they use knife and fork,
cut their meat piece by piece,
then every time switch knife with fork;
it's a wonder they find their mouths with that work.

Necessity is the mother of invention.
Plato

Lake Agassiz

When the ice sheets melted
ten thousand years ago,
their waters formed a giant lake,
its volume greater than the Great Lakes hold.
This lake, confined by giant ice dams,
at various times broke,
sending enormous floods to the Atlantic realm.
It raised the waters in many places
along the shores of seas.
It covered lands where people lived,
expelled them from where they had dwelt many years.
There have been events of similar kind.
Might they be the cause
for begetting flood myths in our minds?

Good tests kill flawed theories;
we remain alive to guess again.
Karl Popper

Terrorist

How depraved must you be
to decapitate a man
you don't even know,
who has never hurt you,
has done nothing
to inflict harm and sorrow,
just fell captive to your sorry spawn.
Once you have died,
with Judgement Day come,
and you walk yawm ad-din
toward paradise to take you in,
may you drop off as-sirat,
your Islamic razor-sharp bridge above Hell.
But I'm certain, poorly schooled as you are,
you've never heard of yawm ad-din,
nor do you know of this bridge, as well.

God is a metaphor for that which transcends
all levels of intellectual thought.
It's as simple as that.
Joseph Campbell

Fear of Dying

haunts the living.
Fear of consciousness, that is.
Fear of what they might find in Hell,
for few in Heaven will ever dwell.
What troubles most, however, is,
that there may lurk only nothingness.

We're so engaged in doing things to achieve purposes of outer
value
that we forget the inner value.
The rapture that is associated with being alive,
is what it is all about.
Joseph Campbell

Almost Rain

Feathery vanes of rain hang suspended
from clouds laden heavy with moisture.
Sometimes billowing, drifting about,
when dispersed they are called jellyfish clouds.
They'd love to moisten the thirsting earth,
but the air below is too hot and dry
for the wispy streaks to make it down.
Thus they float towards earth, these ephemeral veils,
sometimes a colorful display they make.
Pristine and virginal they are,
poetic their name
being called virga.

I once had a sparrow alight on my shoulder for a moment
while I was hoeing in a village garden,
and I felt that I was more distinguished by that circumstance
than I should have been by any epaulet I could have worn.
Henry David Thoreau

Projection

There are times when
a listener interrupts for good reason.
But there are also situations when the one who's spoken-to
interrupts because he projects
what his mind tells him to do.
No listener then, he is certain to know
what the speaker is going to say.
No matter its correctness,
it becomes the one who's spoken-to,
the "victim's," defensive ploy.
Between partners it confirms in the spoken-to's mind
that that which is projected is fact.
But if it's not, and repeated too often,
it's going to destroy a failing pact,
for it frames the speaker,
in the mind of the other,
no matter whether the image held
is factual or not.
For both there's no escaping this terrible trap.

We don't see things as they are;
we see things as we are.
The Talmud

Universal Words

There are such universal words
as "trouble" and "stuff," surely others.
Conveniently, they apply to all "things,"
into which all we're dumping,
when we don't quickly find a specific term
that saves us from this silly lumping.
These days there's a lot of "stuff"
that keeps us in a troubling bubble.
The "thing" is, we don't know at all
how to get out of this "trouble."

We are what we repeatedly do.
Excellence, then, is not an act but a habit.
Aristotle

Snarl

Once, on a safari, I recall,
there rested this group of lions.
Their bodies, prone,
surrounded some bushes
whose shade changed with the moving sun.
When, later, we looked at the pictures we took,
there was a single shot
of a vicious snarl a lioness gave.
Was it true or was it not?
Then, when we viewed it in a movie,
it looked much more benign.
The lioness's snarl was but a yawn,
not an irritated sign.
You just can't trust a single picture you see.
It can distort the truth
of what happened really.

The greatest reward lies in making the discovery;
recognition can add little or nothing to that.
Franz Ernst Neumann

The Bell

There came the time
when a pilgrim I was,
to a village in Würtemberg lands.
There, in the last year of the War,
I'd found peace from the dropping bombs.
First at seven, then eight in nineteen-forty-four,
I had had the run of the place.
One day, I recall, I was taken by elders
to the little village church.
They showed me how to pull the rope
to get the bell to ring,
and once I did, I rose to the heavens,
but ring the bell I did.
Again I stood in the little church,
likely a final time.
A guest book lay in front of me,
waiting for words of mine.
Signing it, I thought it well
to tell other readers that:
Seventy years ago,
I'd rung this very bell.

Happiness is a butterfly, which, when pursued,
is always beyond your grasp,
but which, if you sit down quietly, may alight upon you.
Nathanial Hawthorne

Loss

I have a friend who lost his wife
a couple of years ago.
Gregarious he is, loves the company of women,
but won't give romance a go.
I cannot be certain but don't think I am off,
when I believe he is
with his wife still in love.

Love, which is only an episode in the life of man,
is the entire history of woman's life.
Germaine de Stael

Solutions

With a couple of friends
we gather, in turn, to discuss at our homes
what makes the world churn.
Any subject is right,
we argue well,
and we "solve" many problems
of this world full of hell.
And the following day,
believe it or not,
we find the problems we tackled
are no longer at fault.

Don't judge each day by the harvest you reap,
but by the seeds you plant.
Robert Louis Stevenson

Phobias

My family, especially I, were friends
with an elderly couple next door.
They had a son, a Luftwaffe officer,
who, on vacation, visited there.
A strapping pilot he surely was.
He tried, me, a four-year-old, to toughen up
in nineteen-forty with Hitler's clap-trap.
He grabbed me once,
kicking and screaming,
and held me, poor chap,
over their balcony's balustrade,
three stories up.
Thus, acrophobia looms
whenever I walk a steep, scary slope.
Then, at eleven, we played a game,
to enter a sack, tight as they came.
When I wanted out,
my mates kept me shut
in the narrow, tight, dark, confining sack.
Once more did I scream
until they let me out,
and this was when I learned
what claustrophobia is about.

None are so empty as those who are full of themselves.
Benjamin Whichcote

Solitude

There's solitude and loneliness.
The latter arises when something's amiss.
One can have friends but still be alone,
for the one who is missing
is remote from one's home.
Solitude is fine as it goes,
but loneliness can bring on bitter woes,
which is when the most important person or friend,
is out of reach and not at hand.

What's a friend?
A single soul dwelling in two bodies.
Aristotle

Question

Should I, should I, should I not,
head to Africa once more,
her bush, her savannas my eternal lure?
At seventy-eight my time's running out
to go once more on a walk-about.
I'd love to explore these spaces where
I would meet the wild beasts
in their own living sphere,
where they are at home,
while I must take care.
To walk the bush,
drive the savanna,
paddle the lakes,
the rivers, the swamps.
Most folks do shy from it,
but with day-tripping done,
one always returns to a luxurious camp,
its people most friendly,
food and drinks excellent.
All in all a thrill,
a vacation well spent.

The only way to get rid of a temptation
is to yield to it.
Oscar Wilde

Rhapsody in Blue

Depicting the so beautiful,
the essence of America,
her people from so many lands.
Her vigor, drive, inventiveness,
her nature, pride and, yes, her Jazz.
Back in my teens, in Germany,
I dearly loved this piece already,
George Gershwin's finest composition.
Its passages I used to sing,
jazzed up its rhythms,
made them swing.
And once, in Sweden, I was asked
to sing for friends,
but I declined.
To sing it today
is a thing of the past.

The past is not dead.
In fact, it's not even past.
William Faulkner

Progress

Most of us living
have not the faintest idea,
how we got from there to here.
Not long ago, we in the so-called Western World,
lived rather poorly, ignorant
of much that made this world go 'round.
The same is true, even today.
While poor living faded,
ignorance was left to stay.
The texting generation has no clue
where we came from
and to whom to give its due.
Will smartphones tell of water impure,
of outhouses, poor sanitation,
the cities full of horse manure?
Lives were shorter,
without security in old age.
And writing letters was all the rage.
I could go on, and on, and on,
but what's the use?
Let's hope the progress lasts,
and that the past is ever past.

Opportunities multiply as they are seized.
Sun Tzu

Sentience and Sapiens

Alone on our planet Earth,
and possibly in the universe,
if not, at least the Milky Way,
we, humankind, evolved.
Alone we are,
thus keep on searching,
for minds, alike, to find.
We want to learn if there are others
who can reason, are sapient,
sentient to perceive and feel, are of mind.
It took ages to develop these traits,
and in doing so
we left our earthly fellow-beings behind.
And still we struggle to develop reason,
our desires, wants and feelings,
the subjective conscious experience,
to become less animalian,
beings of a different, more decent kind.

Our knowledge is a torch of smoky pine
that lights the pathway but one step ahead
across a void of mystery and dread ,. . . .
George Santayana, "Sonnet III"

Enough

I couldn't help writing a little bit more,
but enough is enough.
This closes the door.
But I leave it ajar for a teensy bit.
Who knows what may transpire yet?

Do not regret growing old;
many are denied the privilege.
Ogden Nash

Spirit

by Karl May

It was the day the spirit woke,
from waters, dreaming of worlds far removed,
reflecting on the word of the Almighty God,
from which his wondrous promise to him spoke:

I grant you now this image: Earth.
Go there, humanely make it come to be,
so that through love, divine it shall become,
which, from my Father's house, I do send on.

Then, in the east, the light of lights took hold,
life's tide, which everlasting blooms,
and full of wonder was he face-to-face,
the spirit - for the first time - with the face of God.

If

by Rudyard Kipling

If you can keep your head when all about you are losing theirs
and blaming it on you;

If you can trust yourself when all men doubt you,
but make allowance for their doubting too:

If you can wait and not be tired of waiting, or, being lied about,
don't deal in lies, or being hated don't give way to hating,
and yet don't look too good, nor talk too wise;

If you can dream - and not make dreams your master;

If you can think - and not make thoughts your aim;

If you can meet with Triumph and Disaster and treat those
two impostors just the same;

If you can bear to have the truth you've spoken twisted by knaves to
make
a trap for fools, or watch the things you gave your life to, broken,
and stoop and build 'em up with worn out tools;

If you can make one heap of all your winnings and risk it on one turn
of pitch-and-toss, and lose, and start again at your

beginnings,
and never breathe a word about your loss:

If you can force your heart and nerve and sinew to serve your turn
long after they are gone, and so hold on when there is nothing in
you
except the Will which says to them "Hold on!"

If you can talk with crowds and keep your virtue, or walk with Kings-
nor lose the common touch;

If neither foes nor loving friends can hurt you,

If all men count with you, but none too much;

If you can fill the unforgiving minute with sixty seconds' worth
of distance run, Yours is the Earth and everything that's in it.

And - which is more - you'll be a man, my son!

18442205R00126

Made in the USA
San Bernardino, CA
14 January 2015

Pondering What Is

Herbert Windolf

ISBN: 1505540089
ISBN 13: 9781505540086
Library of Congress Control Number: 2014922391
CreateSpace Independent Publishing Platform
North Charleston, South Carolina